Amelia
POETRY

Collection of Classical and Spiritual Poems

Amelia Ventus

Amelia Poetry

Collection of Classical
and
Spiritual Poems

Amelia Ventus

CITI OF
BOOKS

CITIOFBOOKS, INC.
3736 Eubank NE Suite A1
Albuquerque, NM 87111-3579
www.citiofbooks.com

Hotline: 1 (877) 389-2759
Fax: 1 (505) 930-7244

Ordering Information:
Quantity sales. Special discounts are available on quantity purchases by corporations, associations, and others. For details, contact the publisher at the address above.

Printed in the United States of America.

ISBN-13:   Paperback   979-8-89391-411-5
              eBook   979-8-89391-412-2

Library of Congress Control Number: 2024922187

Table of Contents

Pleasantry

It's great to know someone like you
Pleasant ways and attitude

Your kindness would have been enough
You added pleasantries with a tender touch

People like you are so hard to find
I'll forever treasure your being so kind.

NOTES

Life With Jesus

Only a good start makes a good end
Start with Jesus; He's your friend

He's able to lead your path and way
Guiding your footsteps every day

You'll gain a new strength to make you strong
He'll step right in when things go wrong

When your entire world turns misty blue
Depend upon the one who will come through

Life with Jesus leaves no room for doubt
Don't lose your way and let the fire go out

Stay at the feet of Jesus; blessings will never cease
Do it his way and find the pathway to peace.

NOTES

God Can Make Your Moment

What God gives you, he wants you to use it
Embrace your given gifts and don't refuse it
When becoming low-spirited and feeling like nothing
God shows up and you go through something

He wants your best, so he'll do a test
Trusting in God, he always gives moments of rest
He is strengthening your testimony stronger
Though you feel suffering, can't be any longer

With the struggles of life's storms and its pain
Dealing victoriously with life's denials can be a gain
You can have joy; the choice is yours
The world's joy expires and shuts down its doors

Being the best me I can be becomes your lifestyle history
Departure a life of sinning to a life of winning is God's victory
Make the right turn; don't let yourself become lost
God wants to be near you, for he paid at the cross.

NOTES

_____

_____

_____

_____

_____

_____

_____

_____

_____

_____

_____

_____

_____

_____

Thoughtful Moments

I wanted to reveal my sincere love for you, but I didn't
I wanted to share my thoughts, but I couldn't
I wanted to explore a deeper friendship, but I shouldn't
I wanted these meaningful feelings be known, but I wouldn't

I wanted to reach out more for your touch, but I didn't
I wanted to capture more closeness, but I couldn't
I wanted to hold tightly onto your caresses, but I shouldn't
I wanted to set aside these thoughts, but I wouldn't

I wanted to keep telling myself to let go, but I didn't
I wanted to remove these desires, but I couldn't
I wanted to hold onto these moments, but I shouldn't
I wanted to share such great memories, but I wouldn't.

NOTES

Rise Up and Build

Let us rise up and build
And let's do it God's way
Time is now and don't stand still
He'll teach us how to pray

Never let go of God's hand
In it, safety you'll find
God has a simplified plan
To cure a messed-up mind

Going all the way with Jesus
Who will stay with you to the end
Heartaches and troubles may seize us
He'll always be your everlasting friend

Lord, what will you have us to do?
Bright lights and beautiful cities stole our joy
To recover this, joy will help us to know too
Keeping company with Jesus is the greatest ploy

The secret of joy is to worship him
And with him, real victory is yours
The royal road to blessings is not dim
A life with Jesus will surely open doors.

NOTES

Forever Holding

Your embraces are so warm
So warm it brought about fear
Fear to want your touch
The touch to have you near

Struggling with the need to holdback
Holdback feelings that are so strong
Strong to start the mind wondering
Wondering, Can this goodness all be wrong?

Just to see you to exchange a smile
A smile to capture and hold
Hold within and forever keep
Keep within the warmth of my soul

Perhaps there's something more to consider
Considering our friendship has grown
Grown to heights one can't measure
Measuring to where we least have known

Each passing day, thoughtfully are cherished
Cherished with every moment and time
Time given to each precious thought
Thoughts that stay forever on my mind.

NOTES

Soul-Saving

Within this world, life can seem so dark
Jesus stands with an invitation into the ark

When sin and Satan sometime seize us
Don't go down in the hand reach of Jesus

There's no need to get lost in your own house
Your sins can be doused

After meeting the Lord, there's a new song to sing
So much happiness and joy it will bring

Life with Jesus leaves no room for doubt
Hold on to Jesus and don't let the fire go out.

NOTES

Become Revived

Don't let your heart be ripped and torn
Christ is able to calm life's storm

Believing in him gives comfort forevermore
He'll always guide us to an open door

Life doesn't have to become tedious
When you open your heart to the love of Jesus

Don't be lost and weary in your search
The Bible gives us Jesus' mission for the church

So don't lose your way and become a mourner
Become revived and hold up your corner.

NOTES

The Chosen One

You're the one that God uses to guide his people
To follow the pathway to greater wisdom

Each day, he gives you a new revelation
Just so we can enter into his kingdom nation

Helping us with many falls that might prevail
As we follow his Holy Word, we can't fail

Keep a stronghold on his Word even when sad
For the Word strengthens and removes the bad

His written Word and the Holy Spirit leading the way
Revealing God's goodness in all that you say

We can always sing and shout as we run this race
To God be the Glory for his amazing grace.

NOTES

Jesus Loving Us

For so many, LORD, we've all been led
By the wondrous things you've done and said

So many hearts are healed with your mighty touch
Touched by the Holy Spirit that means so much

Miracles after miracles, you perform
Keeping us protected through life's storm

Your works of grace we plainly see
The embrace of your love sets us free

Every single moment, Lord, we've been led
Our peace of life comes from things you've done and said

That's Jesus loving us.

NOTES

A Special Mother

To one who holds the sweetest name
Your love stays and remains the same

Because of you many blessings were cherished
With your love and guidance that could not be banished

Showing and knowing you keep a loving touch
Your caring heart always means very much

You're my all in each given day
Bringing delight to my life in a special way

Sharing each moment of time has brought much pleasure
Each day's journey with you are always treasure.

NOTES

A Lasting Friendship

Now more than before as becoming aware
Of moments that'll always be treasure
The expression of kind words that we share
A gift that brought about so much pleasure.

Awakening at night with thoughts so dear
Torn between sadness and joy within the heart
Somewhat wishing to have you near
Holding this excitement that will not depart.

This friendship blossomed in such a way
Even while suppressing fears of an unseen
Bringing great hopes for a better day
Courage for tomorrow or what the future will bring

Beloved memories are forever on my mind
Keeping these thoughts with so much to gain
What you say and do helps to find
Moments of happiness and lessens any pain.

NOTES

Love

Love can work happiness in it's own way
Finding happiness is a joyous and happy day

A journey hand-in-hand
With problems take a good stand

Depending on where you go and come to know
This happiness will grow and will show.

NOTES

The Connection

Seeking a connection was the goal
Looking for a lost friend from some time ago

Exploring and deepening the depths of my mind
These thoughts began to spin and unwind

Days became weeks before I would find
The wonder of this day only of its kind

Connection settled peacefully into its place
Unspoken emotions warm with embrace

The heart pulsing at an electric pace
Excitedly expecting the ultimate face to face,

This perfect moment came my way
Enclosed in my mind, each hour of the day

Blissfully not knowing what to say
Only everything is possible when you pray

NOTES

In God's Presence

When God's presence is upon you
Pouring of His love shining thru

Words of expressing joy coming from above
Moments embraced by the spirit of His love

While graciously meditating on what would come next
The Holy Spirit led to reading Scripture's text

As the read Word reached the heart
Uplifted spirits began to start

It's such a blessed precious gift to receive
Being in God's presence comes to all who believe.

NOTES

Much Love

The passage of time our friendship grew
Words and smiles shared where an upstart
Friendship became exciting and new
Each day became dear to my heart

Friendship blossomed as days passed by
War with thoughts I quicken to refrain
Coming to grips and asking why
Wanting these feelings to be explained

Moonlit stretches of night meaning so much
Midnight longing to have you near
Wanting to reach out for your touch
Lying and awakening in the wet of tears.

NOTES

Author's Bio

Amelia Ventus, born to the late Andrew and Ida Ventus in the village of Milford, Ohio, currently resides in Pleasant Ridge, Ohio, both of which are suburbs of Cincinnati. She is a graduate of Milford High School and has continued her education at the University of Cincinnati, Xavier University, and earned an Associate of Science degree from Southern Ohio Business College.

Amelia comes from a family of twelve siblings and is the godmother of twins, Marcus and Malcolm. She retired from the Cincinnati Bell Telephone Company, where her career began as a long-distance operator and secretary in the Public Relations Department.

Amelia was very active at the Lincoln Heights Missionary Church, where she was a choir member and taught Primary and Intermediate classes for several years.

Her hobbies include writing, reading, and self-teaching piano by ear. She expresses her gratitude to God for this God-given gift and challenge.

Special thanks to Alexandro Ruiz and Derrick Hogan for their expertise, support, and encouragement in the successful writing of her book

Author Notes

I am so grateful to God for the wisdom, knowledge, and time given to me for moments of meditation and dedication of these writings. Also, my gratitude to my pastor's inspirational and spiritual teaching throughout the years. Your sermon topics were used for these poems.

Thank you to Dr. Elliott Cuff, Dr. Freddie T. Piphus, the late Rev. Lloyd C. Williams, and all the ministers and teachers who have been part of this heartfelt journey. Your inspirational guidance and uplifting spirit have played a crucial role in this gifted endeavor, and I am truly grateful for your support.

Gratefully
Amelia ventus

Acknowledgements

I want to extend my heartfelt thanks to God for granting me the wisdom to write this book. I am also deeply grateful to my family and friends for their unwavering support and encouragement throughout this journey. Your kind words about my poems and the praise for my writing have meant the world to me. Thank you for believing in me and for being such an important part of this experience.

www.ingramcontent.com/pod-product-compliance
Lightning Source LLC
Chambersburg PA
CBHW020813130626
46554CB00006B/2410